Mindset: The Psychology of Success

The First Book in the Series of Mindset for Personal Help, Business, and Leadership

"The Concept of Growth Hacking"

This book is dedicated to my father,

"Those who left us are not absent; they are only invisible: they keep their eyes full of glory focused on ours full of tears."

— Saint Augustine

Table of Contents

Introduction
    What Is Mindset?
    Mindset Theory
    How Is Mindset Formed Throughout Life?
    How Mindset Influences Our Actions and Reactions

Chapter 1: The Fixed Mindset vs. the Growth Mindset
    What Is the Fixed Mindset?
    What Is the Growth Mindset?
    Insecurity and the Fear of Making Mistakes
    The Edison Mentality
    How Worries Are Reprogramming Your Brain
    The Importance of Knowing Oneself

Chapter 2: Growth Hacking
    What Is Growth Hacking?
    How Is Growth Hacking Put Into Practice?
        Self-Discipline
        Visualization
    Benefits of Growth Hacking in Personal Life

Chapter 3: Growth Hacking in Business
    Growth Hacking as a Form of Mindset in Business
    How Growth Hacking Will Lead to Professional Success

Chapter 4: How Mindset Affects Leadership
    Best Mindset for Leadership

Growth Mindset for Non-Traditional Marketing Strategies

Chapter 5: How to Change Your Mindset

Regular Positivity Practice

Facing Fears

Flexible Mindset For Different Situations

1. Getting Out of Debt
2. Feeling Negative

Conclusion

Next Steps

Where to Go From Here to Keep This in Your Professional Life Practice

Introduction

Life is full of challenges and problems; this is one of the things we have to accept that it is unavoidable. If you are faced with obstacles, they have to act with perseverance and persistence in order to stay on track with their journey to success and achievement. By being able to picture what they want, people have achieved goals that they never thought were possible by merely altering their mindset and overcoming bad habits.

Those that are in industries where their success highly relies on their ability to perform tend to naturally showcase better growth mindset behavior due to having more practice from exercising it every day. For example, people in sales tend to showcase growth mindset practice than other occupations because of the targets that they have to meet. People within the sales industry are normally hired due to their motivation to make money.

Due to this motivation, they likely have a goal or target in mind for how much they want to sell within a certain time frame. By having a defined goal, they are driven to do everything they can to reach it and is constantly overcoming obstacles like instant gratification and laziness. If a person is constantly overcoming those obstacles every day, those obstacles slowly start to feel like they aren't there anymore. That's when self-discipline becomes a habit. This is the goal that I want us to get to throughout this book.

You can achieve most of the goals you set for yourself as long as your mindset is there. By being able to picture what they want, people have achieved goals that they never thought were possible simply by altering their mindset and overcoming bad habits.

What Is Mindset?

We will begin by discussing mindset. I am going to define mindset for you first. Mindset is a way of thinking, particularly about things such as talent and intelligence (as well as other qualities). Mindset is defined as whether you think these qualities are fixed or are changeable. If you are a person that believes that traits such as discipline and talent are fixed and unchangeable, or that you are born with them and cannot do anything about them, you would be said to have a fixed mindset. If you believe that these traits are changeable and can grow or diminish over time and with effort, you are said to be a person with a growth mindset. We will discuss these two mindsets in more detail later, but for now, it is essential to know the distinction between the two possible mindsets.

Mindset Theory

The leading mindset theory that exists in society today is that by employing a growth mindset, anyone will be able to change and adjust their traits. What this means is that if a person is able to change their mindset into a growth mindset, then their traits will be changeable. The longer you allow yourself to remain in a fixed mindset, the longer you will be left with the unchangeable traits that you were born with.

How Is Mindset Formed Throughout Life?

Your mindset is formed without your knowledge when you are very young. Your mindset was formed without your input due to a variety of factors. These factors are the following:

- Parental Guidance and Opinions
- Family Members
- Environmental and Societal Factors
- Teachers and Authorities

- The Media

How Mindset Influences Our Actions and Reactions

The mindset you employ has many effects on your life. So many effects that you likely don't even notice how far-reaching they are. Your mindset is able to influence your attitude about any and all situations that you find yourself in and what you attribute these situations to, or what you attribute the fact that you are in these situations to. Your mindset can influence your decision-making and in turn, the way that your life turns out or unfolds. The decisions you make influence the other decisions you make after that, and eventually. The mindset you hold will influence every area of your life since your mindset is the basis for your decisions, your thoughts, and your reactions to situations.

Chapter 1: The Fixed Mindset vs. the Growth Mindset

In this chapter, we are going to look at mindset. We will begin by exploring the two possible types of mindsets and what characterizes each of them, before looking at how each type of mindset can influence your life.

What Is the Fixed Mindset?

The first type of mindset that we will look at is the Fixed Mindset. As you learned in the introduction to this book, a fixed mindset is a way of viewing traits and characteristics. If a person has a fixed mindset, they see a person's traits as fixed and unchangeable.

If a person believes that their traits are not able to be changed, they remain stuck with the traits that they were born with and will not attempt to change them or improve upon them as they believe it cannot be done. For example, "I was born an athlete" or "I was not born a singer." These two examples are ways that a person with a fixed mindset would see the traits of athleticism and the ability to sing. They would not believe that these traits can be changed or improved upon, so they attribute a person's traits to things that they were born with or not born with.

What Is the Growth Mindset?

The 'growth mindset' is a term that was coined by Carol Dweck, who is a renowned professor at multiple universities including Columbia University, Harvard University and the University of Illinois. Her research with Angela Lee Duckworth stated that intelligence is not a key indicator of success. In fact, they believed that success depends on whether or not the person has a growth mindset. A fixed mindset is when a person believes that their intelligence and skills are a fixed trait. They have what they have and that's it. This makes the person highly concerned with what skills and intelligence they currently have and they do not focus on what they can gain. Therefore, their activities are limited to the capacity that they think they have. However, those with growth mindsets understand that skills and intelligence is something that can be developed and learned throughout the course of their life. This can be done through education, training, or simply just even passion. They understand that their brain is a muscle that can be 'worked out' to grow stronger.

Knowing this, it is important that you employ a growth mindset. Every single skill you have and your intelligence can be improved by putting in the effort to do so. Famous public figures of success like Oprah Winfrey, Steve Jobs, and Bill Gates all employed a growth mindset by overcoming every obstacle that got in the way. Rather than succumbing to defeat, they worked and discovered innovative ways to overcome previous failures and found success at the end. Think about what mindset you have right now. If you already have a growth mindset, you simply need to continue practicing it while being proactive about avoiding obstacles and overcoming failures. If you think you are someone with a fixed mindset, change it right now. Believe me when I tell you that intelligence and skills can be improved upon with time and hard work. If you don't believe me, just try it. Pick a random skill. This could be knitting, programming, jogging, or anything that can be learned. Set goals for yourself and begin learning something new. If you are able to take something that you have zero skill in and become proficient in it, you have just proved to yourself that growth mindsets are real and fixed mindsets only hold you back from success.

Insecurity and the Fear of Making Mistakes

An important concept I want you to understand is that failures are welcome when you are practicing self-discipline or when incorporating a new mindset into your life. Do not begin your journey of increasing self-control, thinking that you aren't going to fail. That is only going to discourage you from picking yourself back up. There will be days where you stay in bed instead of going to the gym to improve upon your athleticism, or you decide to eat a double cheeseburger instead of choosing a healthier option in order to improve upon your body type. Having failures is entirely okay as long as you learn from them and find a way to overcome them the next time around. Consistency is what will solidify a new mindset in your brain and in your everyday life.

The Edison Mentality

This is where the 'Edison Mentality' comes in. Thomas Edison truly believes that his success was inevitable. He made sure to align all his goals with what his passions were. This is not to say that he had a fixed mindset, very much the opposite, in fact. Because he had a growth mindset, he made sure to find opportunities to improve upon his skills despite failure or mistakes, because he knew that his skills and his traits could be improved upon if he continued to work towards his goals. This created a powerful sense of motivation and optimism that had a positive effect on everyone around him. This included his family, friends, customers, coworkers, investors, and ultimately, the entire nation. He didn't give up the first time he failed on his journey. He created innovative ways to overcome the obstacles he was faced with. He wasn't disappointed when he faced a problem that halted his progress. He embraced it with open arms because he EXPECTED it. Expect yourself to fail but create a plan that will help you overcome it. That is how you can use failure to teach yourself more self-discipline.

In fact, permanent failure is usually caused by low self-discipline and a fixed mindset. That is the failure you don't want. You want to encounter failures that motivate you to grow and increase your self-control and innovative thinking. If you have low self-discipline, even if you promised your workout buddy to meet you at the gym in the morning, you still won't go because you don't value your commitment to the gym and deep down you do not believe that you will be able to change the body that you were born with anyway.

The one thing that sets most people back from reaching their goals is not knowing how to deal with failures and adversity. Failure is a part of the process. Don't fool yourself by believing that you won't face failure along the way. Everybody does, it's a part of the process. The difference between people who find success and those who don't is simply that those who did were able to learn from their failures, grow, and overcome it. When you are faced with adversity, you must forgive yourself for any mistakes you have made and move forward. Failures and mistakes are a part of the journey. Separate yourself from it and keep moving forward. Do what you can to grow and heal so you can come back stronger than before.

Even if a person has all the best intentions and the most well-made plans, sometimes they will fall short. Avoiding failure altogether is impossible. Everyone will have their ups and downs, their successes, and their failures. The key to overcoming the failures that you will face is to simply keep moving forward. If you stumble on your journey of changing any of your traits or developing a new mindset, instead of giving up altogether, acknowledge what caused it, learn from it, and then move on. Don't let yourself get caught up in frustration, anger, or guilt because these emotions are the ones that will de-motivate you and get in the way of your future progress. Learn from the mistakes you have made and be comfortable with forgiving yourself. Once you have done that, you can get your head back in the game and start where you left off.

How Worries Are Reprogramming Your Brain

When a person is experiencing negative emotions like anxiety, fear, worry, or stress, they are performing negative visualizations. This is a type of visualization that happens unconsciously where the person is not aware that they are negatively visualizing, but it is still a type of visualizing, nonetheless. Every time a person stresses or worries about something, they often suffer from having anxiety or fear about what they think may happen in the future. They are actually in a moment of visualizing negative events. In addition, in that moment, the person is actually rewiring their own brain in limiting ways. Just like how a person's brain can be reprogrammed and rewire to build/improve positive and helpful habits, which you understand if you have a. growth mindset, it is also possible that your traits can be rewired in a negative direction, due to worry and obsessing over your fears of failure.

Every time a person indulges in the worries that they're in at the moment, they are building on the existing neural pathways within their brain. Due to this, every time a person envisions something negative, it causes negative worries much easier. When a person is visualizing negative events, it can make a person feel uneasy or anxious at that moment. A person's subconscious mind can't actually distinguish the difference between what it actually sees and a visualization. Due to this, the person's brain processes those events as if it's a physical action that they have performed. This results in the neural networks forming in their brain which creates new beliefs, habits and perspectives. Ultimately, the person is effectively building new patterns by rewiring their brain to support all the things that they have negatively envisioned. When a person does that, they are building patterns of behavior and skills that aren't helpful to their growth in a positive direction. The more frequently a person thinks about this negative pattern, the easier it is for their mind to keep replaying that negative pattern repeatedly until the action of worrying becomes a habit that is triggered when a person faces any level of uncertainty or fear. How does this relate to a growth mindset? You may be asking. If you are focused on the fear of failure and the worries that plague your mind, you will be stuck in a fixed mindset, unable to escape from the fear and the worry. If you hope to change your mindset, you must be able to break away from your fear of failure and open your mind to change. Once you can do this, you can begin to make changes in a positive direction and you can begin to achieve your goals by changing your traits.

In addition to this, when a person worries about certain things, those things have a higher chance of manifesting within their life. This happens because when a person focuses on negative things, they are doing it using the Reticular Activating System. This person's brain is searching for anything it could around them that would support those worries. Due to this, everything a person sees will then validate all the things that they worry about. In addition, every time a person makes bad decisions or choices based on their flawed perspective, it leads to them have their worries manifested into their real world. On the other hand, by employing a growth mindset, you are able to see things which instead validate your goals and the traits you wish to develop. Once you can do this, your brain will more easily look for ways to achieve and improve this.

The Importance of Knowing Oneself

Knowing yourself is very important when it comes to your mindset. By recognizing which sort of mindset you possess, this will help you to understand your actions and your reactions, as well as your thought processes.

Another reason why it is important to know yourself is because of something called your inner critic. Your inner critic is that voice that criticizes you and tells you negative things about yourself, such as "you're too dumb; you'll never get your dream job." Or "they'll never pick you out of all of the other people in this room." These are typical examples of things that you may hear your inner critic telling you. Your inner critic is fearful and worried and does not want you to put yourself out there or step outside of your comfort zone. The inner critic has an intense fear of making mistakes, and it wants to avoid failure at all costs. By having the self-awareness to recognize when your inner critic is telling you negative things, you will be able to stop listening to it and consciously choose a growth mindset. Choosing a growth mindset will also help you to realize that you can change the degree to which your inner critic has control over you and your life.

In our world today, it is a cultural norm to believe that self-criticism will bring motivation to achieving goals and avoiding procrastination. This type of self-criticism functions under the false belief that when a person realizes that their actions or performance isn't good enough, they'll want to change. Our inner-critic is also guilty for giving us a sense of control, but not in the right places. We also use our own judgmental thoughts as a way of coping with emotions like shame, fear, and the unknown. Over time, these comments made by yourself or other people manifest inside of you and eventually become your own unique "inner-critic". To put it in its purest form, your inner critic is the persistent negative self-talk that keeps us stuck.

A person's inner-critic plays a huge role when it comes to things like mental health, self-esteem, and mindset. We notice that our inner-critics usually live in a world that is black and white, a world with very little room for grey areas. Inner-critics share words with you, such as, "You should just give up." Or "What makes you think you'll succeed?" Instead of creating an open space that allows for mistakes, growth, and development, our inner critics cause us to question our worth which makes it difficult for us to have the right mindset to complete needed tasks.

For some people, their inner critic is reflective of a voice from their past. It could be their mother, father, the boss that fired them. For others, it could simply be their own voice talking down to them. Often times, anybody who makes an offhand comment at you may cause you take it so deeply that those words become a part of your identity and your inner voice. This can have profound effects on your mindset over time, especially if this happens to a person in childhood.

It is necessary to train your inner critic so that it does not control you. If you are able to train your inner critic, you will be in control of your mindset.

Knowing yourself will help you to see your own negative thoughts that your inner critic feeds you in its repetitive cycle of self-detriment. By knowing yourself, you can avoid judging yourself harshly, and you can begin to put this negative inner voice aside in order to overcome fears and change your mindset.

Unfortunately, the type of communication that our inner critic uses to communicate with us is anxiety-provoking and shaming which actually creates something that is the complete opposite of motivation. It triggers us to stay safe and to avoid situations or new ways of thinking that may be scary at first. Avoidance with the goal of reducing anxiety is not the same as having the motivation to change. If the messages that our inner-critic is telling us are often shameful, such as "why are you so lazy?" or "what's wrong with you?" we often become paralyzed, unable to change anything and unable to see the next steps in any given situation. When people feel shame, they feel that there is something that is so flawed within them that they don't feel worthy of connections with other people. Shame is the emotion that disconnects us from other people and teaches us to feel alone. As humans, it is within our nature to crave a certain level of human connection. When we often feel feelings of shame caused by our inner critic, these feelings make us want to withdraw from the world and further trigger avoidance behaviors like procrastination as a way to soothe or comfort ourselves. Ultimately, shame and self-criticism work hand in hand to prevent us from doing the things that we need to do in order to reach our goals or simply just to take care of ourselves.

Awareness, or knowing yourself, is the first step that needs to be taken in order to recognize your inner critic and reshape your mindset from a fixed mindset to a growth mindset. Try to pay attention the next time you are feeling distracted, numb, or fearful. Try to identify when your inner critic is the one dictating your thoughts and actions and consciously choose a growth mindset instead. Try to find the situation where your inner critic awakens. Knowing yourself and being able to self-reflect allows you to dig deep and identify the most vulnerable feelings you have, especially in times of fear or insecurity. By trying to protect you, your inner critic is holding you back from meeting your full potential and being able to break free from this begins with knowing yourself. We must break away from this inner critic in order to achieve our goals, change our mindset and accomplish new and difficult things.

Chapter 2: Growth Hacking

In this chapter, I will introduce a new concept. This concept is Growth Hacking. This concept is similar to the growth mindset which we have been discussing so far in this book. We will begin by defining what growth hacking is. Then I will outline how putting this into practice can help you in a number of different areas of your life.

What Is Growth Hacking?

Growth Hacking is a relatively new term. This term came along with the age of start-ups. This term is something that has the potential to change your life in a business sense as well as a personal sense. A man named Sean Ellis is the person who developed this word ten years ago. This man was a businessman who wanted to develop this term as a way of sharing his thoughts about how to achieve great things in business in the age of start-ups. This term came about because of a need to redefine the way that people do business in the age of technology. This term comes down to one basic idea that is completely necessary when working for or beginning your own start-up. This word is *growth*. The term can be used to describe a job title, a person or a company by calling them a "growth hacker." A growth hacker is a person who works toward growth in every sense of the word. A growth hacker is interested in hacking systems (in a figurative sense) in order to develop new ways of growing a business in terms of marketing, sales, finance and human resources.

How Is Growth Hacking Put Into Practice?

Growth Hacking requires not only a growth mindset, but it also requires the tools to put it into practice in order to make it a part of your life. How can you begin to put this into practice? You may be wandering through something called Self-Discipline.

Self-Discipline

Life is full of challenges and problems; this is one of the things we have to accept that it is unavoidable. When you are faced with obstacles, you must face them and act with perseverance and persistence in order to stay on track with your journey to success and achievement of your goals. In order to rise above these obstacles and maintain your growth mindset, you will require self-discipline. In this section, we will look into self-discipline further in order to better understand how it will unlock the secret to maintaining your growth mindset and putting it into practice.

If you possess self-discipline, it often leads to building other positive components of yourself, such as self-confidence and self-esteem. Having a good balance of these components in your life leads to higher happiness and satisfaction.

However, if you lack self-discipline, it often leads to negative things like failure, health, loss, obesity, relationship problems, and many other undesirable things. Self-discipline is a useful skill that you can learn to overcome negative habits such as eating disorders, addictions, smoking, and drinking. Everyone requires it in order to make themselves exercise, develop new skills, study, self-improvement, meditation, and even spiritual growth.

Like we mentioned above, many people understand all the benefits of having strong self-discipline, but not many actually do the work to develop and strengthen it. Self-discipline is a skill just like any other. You have the ability to strengthen it as long as you keep practicing it. In this way, it also takes a growth mindset to be able to develop and improve your level of self-discipline since it must be understood as a changeable trait. You can specifically focus on building your self-discipline skills through the use of exercises and training in order to remain in control of your thoughts and actions, as your mindset has great influence over these two things.

What Is Self-Discipline?

Self-discipline is one of the most useful and vital skills that everyone will benefit from having. This skill is crucial in pretty much every area of a person's life. Although most people know how important this skill is, not many take the time to practice strengthening it. The common belief regarding self-discipline is living a strict and limited lifestyle while being harsh to oneself. However, self-discipline simply means self-control and building the inner strength to control yourself, your behavior, and your reactions.

Self-discipline is the power that a person has in order to be able to stick with their decisions and to follow them through without changing their minds. This is one of the most important conditions before one can achieve their goals. Having self-discipline allows people to persevere with their decisions and continues to plan to accomplish their goals. Self-discipline can also be known as inner strength, which helps people overcome obstacles like laziness, procrastination and even addictions.

One of the main traits of self-discipline is the ability to deny instant gratification and pleasure in return for greater gain, which requires a person to put in effort and time to achieve. Most people know that self-discipline is one of the most crucial components when it comes to success. Here is how self-discipline expresses itself:

- Self-control
- Perseverance
- The ability to not give up even when faced with obstacles and failure
- The ability to resist temptations or distractions

- The ability to keep trying until you accomplish the goal you've set

The Importance of Seeing Self-Discipline From a Growth Mindset

Self-Discipline is a learned skill; it is not an innate characteristic. What does this mean? I will start by defining these two terms for you. A learned skill, as I am sure you can imagine, is something that you can learn and develop in order to possess. This is the opposite of an innate characteristic, which is something that you are born with. There are some characteristics that you are born with such as the color of your eyes or certain aspects of your personality such as being stubborn or brave.

The other difference is that one is a skill, and the other is a characteristic. Skills are things that you can study, practice and improve upon. Skills are things like communication or cooking. A characteristic is something that you possess that you do not have much control over. You can work on things like becoming braver, but for the most part, you are born a brave person, or you are not.

Knowing this fact can help you to feel empowered and hopeful. If you struggle with self-discipline, knowing that it is a skill that can be learned and honed over time means that this will not remain something that you struggle with anymore. By reading this book, you are already taking the first steps to changing your life by becoming a more self-disciplined person. If this were an innate characteristic, this would mean that it would be difficult for you to change.

Visualization

The second way that we are going to discuss for you to put Growth Hacking into practice is through visualization. Visualization is a technique that can be used for a variety of purposes, but it has been shown to be extremely useful in helping people to achieve their goals and learn new things. In our case, visualization can help you to put this new mindset into practice, in order to help solidify it in your brain.

The process of visualization activates the Reticular Activating System in your brain, and this helps a human to remember more details about a situation such as awareness of the events, opportunities, and other people that are related to the goals which they are visualizing. When the person then goes to perform the activities that they visualized in real life, the Reticular Activating System fires up again, leading the person to make conscious and subconscious choices that will help them to achieve the goals that they visualized. This then helps them to achieve their goals in reality. Due to this, you can use visualization as an empowering and helpful tool to achieve any goals you wish to accomplish.

In this section, we will be taking a look at four different types of visualization techniques that a person can use to help improve their life. These techniques include:

- Mastering a new skill
- Healing your mind and body
- Achieving your goals
- Creating an action plan

Mastering a New Skill

Visualization can be used to not only learn a new skill but to master it as well. Visualization is really effective in mastering new skills because of the fact that the brain fires in exactly the same ways when it is visualizing an experience as it is does when the body is actually going through the experience. In this way, visualization helps to prepare the brain for the actual experience, kind of like a dry run. Someone who is visualizing the skill has the same brain activity as when they physically do that skill.

Let's take a look at a study that an Australian psychologist did that studied the effectiveness of visualization regarding a person's ability to do free throws in basketball.

This psychologist chose three groups of students at random who have never tried visualization before. The first group practiced the skill of free throwing for 20 days straight. The second group only practiced free throws twice, once on the very first day and once on the last day. The third group did the same. However, the third group spent half an hour every day visualizing themselves practicing free throws. If they had "missed" in their visualized free throw, they "practiced" getting it right the next time. On the last day of this study, the psychologist measured how the participants improved using percentages. The group that got physical practice every day improved their free throws by 24%. The second group that only practiced twice did not improve at all. However, the third group who had practiced just as much as the second group did 23% better, nearly the same as the first group. At the end of this experiment, the psychologist published a paper that was about how most effective visualization happens when the visualizer is able to see what they are doing. In other words, the ones that practiced visualizing the free-throw actually 'felt' the basketball in their hands and 'saw' it go through the hoop and have heard it 'bounce'.

The relevance here is that this study shows the profound impact that practicing visualization has on a person's success. If you visualize yourself practicing a skill that you would like to improve upon or that you would like to learn, you will be better prepared to act out this skill in your real life. This also makes this new skill more easily accessible by your brain. For example, if you are practicing your new Growth Mindset through visualization, then your brain will remember this new way of thinking the next time you go into the world and will begin to see the world through this lens.

How to Practice Visualization

You can use visualization to improve upon any skills you want to learn or improve upon. In this section, I will outline for you the steps to begin practicing visualization. Make sure that you try to utilize all of your five senses when you are visualizing. Below are five simple steps that you can follow to begin practicing visualization;

1. Choose a skill that you are interested in mastering.
2. Identify what your real-world proficiency level is in this skill.
3. Visualize yourself doing this skill in as much detail as you can using all five senses.
4. Repeat this visualization for 11 days at 20 minutes per day.
5. Perform this skill physically and keep track of measuring your improvement. Continue visualizing while doing that skill in real life if you are not satisfied with the results

Creating an Action Plan

If you are feeling overwhelmed or stressed, creating a plan of action using visualization can help you relax and motivate you to take action. This technique is most effective if you use it before you go to bed so you can start planning the next day's work. However, you can use this technique throughout the day if you have 10 minutes of free time.

Below are three simple steps on how to do this:

1. Calm yourself down, and make sure you are feeling relaxed. Sit down as it will help you get some rest from whatever you were doing before.

2. Close your eyes and start to visualize which things specifically that you want to accomplish for tomorrow. Now, visualize those actions that you'd like to do in as much detail as you can and then ask yourself these questions below:

    a. How do I want to feel?

    b. How will I interact with others?

    c. What specific actions do I want to take?

    d. What do I want?

    e. What obstacles will I potentially face?

    f. How will I overcome obstacles?

    g. What do I want to achieve?

3. The reality here is that people are not able to predict all the things that might happen to them. When events happen unexpectedly, they can often ruin any plans that have been put in place. However, good planning isn't about planning around all possible obstacles, but it is more about adapting to the obstacles that life gives you. When you keep this in mind, you must affirm with yourself at the end of your session with "this or something better will come my way". By giving yourself affirmation, you are keeping your mind open to endless possibilities. This will result in you be more ready and okay with making adjustments when unexpected things happen to you.

This process is definitely not a foolproof plan. However, this visualization will help you envision possible situations that might happen. These scenarios will allow you to be able to make better decisions as you continue to work towards your goals.

Achieving Your Goals

This visualization technique is the most important one when it comes to strengthening self-discipline. By using the technique of visualization for setting goals brings a lot of value, but this technique does come with one major drawback. The most popular form of visualization is goal setting. Most people have definitely used visualization pertaining to their goals at one time or another. However, this technique may not have worked for them due to one critical flaw. This flaw is that when people are visualizing their goals, they only focus on visualizing their end goal and nothing in between. They see within their mind's a big and flashy awesome goal that's going to be rainbows and butterflies. Yes, they are experiencing this using all of their sensories but they simply open their eyes after the visualization feeling very inspired. However, this type of motivation is extremely short-lived because the next time this person faces an obstacle, it immediately deflates their motivation.

When this happens, people feel the visualize their goal again to create more motivation. However, because nothing happens every time they visualize their goal, their motivation doesn't grow either. In fact, every time a person hits an obstacle, and they try the process of visualization again, their motivation becomes weaker every time, and they start to lose more and more energy.

The mistake that these people are making is that they are not properly visualizing their goals. They only see the destination, but they don't understand that achieving a goal takes much more than just that. Achieving a goal is part of a journey that is full of emotional highs and lows, wins and losses, and a journey of ups and downs. Due to this, these are the things that a person would also need to include in their visualization.

When a person visualizes their end goal, it is very effective in creating that desire and hunger. However, the proper way to use visualization is only to spend 10 percent of your time visualizing the end goal and spending the rest of the visualization time thinking about HOW you will achieve your goals and overcome challenges. In some ways, it's similar to the form of visualization planning that we just discussed.

A person's end goal helps keep inspiration running in the long term, but it is the journey that helps a person stay motivated in the short term. The way to maximize the time spent on achieving small goals to get to your end goal, you must visualize those as well.

Below are five steps that you can follow to achieve this visualization:

1. Get yourself to a quiet place and sit down and close your eyes. Start to visualize your end goal. Imagine yourself experiencing and living this goal using all five of your senses.
2. Slowly take steps backward from your end goal and start to visualize the process that you took that lead to you achieving your end goal. Imagine all the problems that you faced that put you back; however, you can see yourself finding solutions to those problems. Continue visualizing until you are back to the present moment.
3. Now, move forward with time and visualize how you took on opportunities that helped you overcome your problems.

4. At the end of this visualization, take a few moments to send your future self some positive energy for their journey.

5. When you exit the visualization, emotionally detach from the outcome of your goal. The thing that can hold you back is if you are having an emotional attachment to a specific result. Instead, try to stay open-minded and be flexible for what's to come on your journey.

You can use visualization using those steps on a daily or weekly basis. Weekly sessions can be as long as 30 minutes, and you can keep your daily sessions shorter so they are between 5 - 10 minutes. However, be sure that you are using your daily sessions to visualize the next steps of achieving your goal for the upcoming week. This will help you continue moving forward to reach your goal. After that, you can use your weekly visualizations using the five steps above.

Benefits of Growth Hacking in Personal Life

Now that you know how to put growth hacking into practice, you will be able to begin trying this in your own life. We will shortly discuss how you can use this in your professional or your business life, but first, we will discuss how this will benefit you in your personal life.

Growth hacking came about in response to a need in the business world, but that does not mean that it cannot be employed in your personal life. If you are able to employ a growth mindset in your personal life, you will also be able to use growth hacking in your personal life. As long as you can employ this mindset, you will then be able to approach any problem or challenge in your personal life without the fear of failure and insecurity. As you now know, fear of failure can hold you back from success as it prevents you from seeing your potential for growth. If you have a growth mindset and you can put your fear of failure aside, you will then be able to make changes in your life that will be beneficial to your personal life. For example, if you face a challenge in your personal life such as balancing a variety of commitments on the same day, you will be able to exercise your growth hacking skills to come up with new and innovative possible solutions that will help you to overcome this challenge in a new way.

Another way that this can benefit you in your personal life is that by having a growth mindset, you will be able to approach the concept of growth hacking from this perspective. You will then be able to understand that you can develop your growth hacking skills in order to become a better growth hacker, which will help you to become a better growth hacker over time. By changing your mindset, everything else will improve.

Chapter 3: Growth Hacking in Business

We have previously discussed how growth hacking and a growth mindset will benefit you in terms of your own approach to life and your own traits. In this chapter, we will look at how you can put this into practice in business and in your professional life.

Growth hacking involves trying new things and breaking free from the traditional ways of doing things that won't serve the business world in the same way that they used to because of the immense role that technology plays in business today. Sean Ellis saw this coming ten years ago and developed this term to explain to people what he was looking for in employees and partners of his start-up. He wanted growth, and he knew that they would have to find new ways to grow as technology was rapidly developing.

Growth Hacking as a Form of Mindset in Business

From the definition of growth hacking, as defined above, you can surely see how this way of conducting business requires a growth mindset. If a person has a fixed mindset, they will face great difficulty finding new and innovative ways of growing their business by promoting it, selling their goods or services, or employing new people who share their vision. By understanding that traits and common practices can be changed and improved upon, a person will be able to create new ideas and practices. A person with a fixed mindset would greatly limit themselves in terms of being able to imagine new scenarios and practices, as they would believe that they are already equipped with all of the traits that they were born with. For example, a person with a fixed mindset may think to themselves "I am not creative." By thinking this way, they will limit themselves when it comes to thinking of new ways of tackling problems in business and in growing a start-up. On the other hand, if someone sees themselves as someone who is not inherently creative but who possesses the potential to grow and change, they will better understand the ability of a business to grow and change as well.

How Growth Hacking Will Lead to Professional Success

If you are able to begin practicing growth hacking, you will surely see professional success. This is due to the fact that you will see things in an entirely different way than the other people you work alongside. Most people approach business in a traditional sense, but by employing growth hacking using the techniques that we discussed, you will be able to make yourself an invaluable asset in your job title and your company in general.

Chapter 4: How Mindset Affects Leadership

When it comes to being a good leader, your mindset will lead to your success or your failure. To lead other people, you will need to understand that you will be dealing with many personality types and people with different mindsets. Being able to be a good leader involves a variety of different traits, but more importantly, it involves the ability to change your mindset and adapt. Being able to adapt requires a growth mindset. As you now know, your mindset affects every part of your life, but especially your ability to be a leader.

Further, if you would not consider yourself to be a natural-born leader, you will be able to develop this trait and improve upon it if you possess a growth mindset.

Best Mindset for Leadership

In this section, we are going to look at the traits that make a good leader. This will help you as these traits, along with a growth mindset, will make you a great business leader who will be able to employ growth hacking to make your business or your start-up grow in no time.

As humans, the traits we desire in a leader are somewhat universal. We want to feel like we can trust the person, but also that they will speak up and advocate for us when need be. We want to feel like they listen to us and understand us, while also being prepared to make decisions on our behalf that will benefit us. We want them to be the confident and self-assured face that represents us but also a relatable one. While it may seem impossible to achieve all of these different things at once, I assure you it is possible. We as humans have a difficult time deciphering real confidence from performed confidence, and we like to believe that the leaders we respect are on a pedestal while still being relatable enough that we trust them. This all comes down to showing confidence and certainty while voicing understanding and concern.

When it comes to a leader, everyone wants someone that is confident in an area where most are not. Where most feel fear and uncertainty, the leader feels confidence and security in their choices. They are not over-confident, however, as this makes people fear naivety. Confidence is often underestimated as a tool for leadership. Yes, the choices a leader makes on behalf of their people are important, but the people want someone to believe in, and they will not believe in someone that does not appear to believe in themselves.

In order to possess these traits, one must possess a growth mindset, especially if they would not consider themselves to be a natural leader.

Growth Mindset for Non-Traditional Marketing Strategies

We are going to look at how you can use a growth mindset to practice growth hacking to develop non-traditional marketing strategies. Using growth hacking will help you to come up with many innovative and non-traditional marketing strategies, but I will give you some examples of non-traditional marketing strategies in order to show you the kinds of strategies that could be developed from this type of mindset.

1. Begin using social media and reach your clients or consumers that way
2. Begin a podcast to reach your consumers on a deeper level by connecting with them
3. Make a smartphone app for your business to reach consumers

4. Give your clients and consumers a way to reach out to you
5. Develop interactive marketing installations for your clients and consumers to learn about you
6. Use non-traditional vehicles to get your message across

Chapter 5: How to Change Your Mindset

Now that you understand the different possible mindsets and the ways that these mindsets can benefit you in your personal and your professional life, we are going to talk about how you can begin to change this mindset for the better. If you are a person who has a fixed mindset, it may be hard for you to understand that it is even possible to change your mindset. I assure you, however, that it is. You will realize this shortly when you begin to change your mindset from a fixed into a growth mindset.

The first step to changing your mindset is understanding this fact- that your mindset can be changed. Without this, you will be stuck in your fixed mindset forever.

Regular Positivity Practice

Numerous research studies have recently found that positive thinking brings a lot of benefits to a person's health. It has the ability to reduce a person's stress levels, improve their mental health and their physical health. Research studies have found that optimists tend to be more successful compared to pessimists. There was a research study that focused on the success of a few salespeople. They found that the more optimistic salespeople made 88% more sales than the pessimistic salespeople. They found that optimistic salespeople were less likely to quit their jobs and or give up during stressful work times. They were also more likely to describe a positive future when it came to their sales careers. This makes a lot of sense really. Having a more positive mindset at work prevents you from giving up and motivates you to work harder. It goes without saying that those who try harder than others and refusing to give up will be more successful than those that give up at the first hint of failure.

Facing Fears

Lifestyle changes may be seemingly simple, but they are actually very powerful tools when it comes to changing a fixed mindset. In some people's cases, a lifestyle change is all they may need to change this. Facing your fears is one way that this can be done. In this section, we will look at how to face your fears to make changes in your mindset and begin to employ growth hacking.

Fear is powerful, helpful, and human emotion. It is the feeling that alerts us when we are in the presence of danger and has been crucial in keeping our species alive. There are two types of responses when it comes to fear; biochemical and emotional. The biochemical response is the universal response of fear, while an emotional response is specific to the individual. When humans are confronted with a perceived threat, our bodies will react in specific ways. These physical reactions include increased heart rate, sweating, and high adrenaline levels. Just like how anxiety activates our fight or flight response, fear does too. This is where our body prepares itself to run away or enter combat. These reactions are all biochemical and are an automatic response that has been crucial to our survival.

Fear often holds people back from trying new things as they are either afraid they will fail or have a bad experience.

1. *Change your perspective.*

If an individual is only focusing on the negative things that will happen if confronted by their fear, it will become difficult to move on from it. Instead, changing your perspective by talking to other people and exchanging experiences can help you realize what other opportunities lie ahead once you overcome your fear. Focus on the positive and think about why you want to move toward and past what you fear.

2. *Question your fears.*

People who suffer from phobias or irrational fears start to take their experience with their fear as evidence of permanent and frightening fear. However, the smart thing to do would be to question your fears and what they are based upon. Sit down and think back to what evidence you may have in your memories that lead to this fear of yours. When you identify that situation, try to look at it from a new perspective rather than looking at them in the same way. Our minds often jump to conclusions or create patterns based on little evidence or experiences, so by questioning our perspective of fear, we may be able to realize that you were looking at it all wrong this whole time.

3. **Don't push your fear away.**

When people try to deny their fears, they try to push it out of their lives and to not think about it, which then causes it to grow stronger. Instead, accept your fear and let the discomfort take over you but after a while, your fear begins to lose steam and becomes a lot smaller in comparison to before. Then, it becomes a lot easier to think of constructive and clear thoughts.

4. **Take just one step.**

Most people that are heavily affected by fears think that taking action means taking one big and risky leap to overcome that fear. However, thinking about this one big action creates apprehension that often leads to more fear and towards not taking any actions at all. Instead, take just one small step today. Pick up the phone and dial a friend or family for help or just simply read over some exercises to manage your fear. Start small to get the ball rolling.

Flexible Mindset For Different Situations

We will now look at some situations where you will need to employ different mindsets to practice growth hacking and develop new ways to deal with these situations.

1. Getting Out of Debt

A good example that a lot of people can relate to is striving to become debt-free. In our society in the present day, millions of people are crippled by student debt, credit card debt, mortgage loans and many other types of debt. If one of your goals is to become debt-free so you can start saving for a comfortable retirement, you must start building the skills and habits for it. Those who simply say "I'm just bad with money!" or "I just love shopping too much!" are employing a fixed mindset where they are making assumptions about themselves regarding their inability to save money. Throw that mindset away and turn it into a growth mindset. Change negative phrases into positive ones such as "I've been bad with money in the past but I am going to learn to be more responsible with it" or "I love shopping but from now on I will budget for it instead".

2. Feeling Negative

When you are feeling negative and just can't seem to get back to your growth mindset, there are things that you can do to combat this. This is most likely due to your inner critic becoming over-active and taking over your thoughts. It can be scary to slip into old ways, but this is not forever, and in this section, I will show you how to deal with this.

The first step you need to take to tame your inner critic is to simply just be aware of it. By being aware of it, you will need to be curious. Most people in modern-day society passively move through their lives. Due to how fast-paced things have become nowadays, if we don't give our thoughts and feelings the attention it needs, we tend to forget about them. Even though everybody feels numerous emotions daily, they don't acknowledge them every time. Instead, people have learned to simply react to everything and turn on auto-pilot. When we do this, we don't question or evaluate the downsides to the actions and decisions we are making.

Living on auto-pilot is the easiest option for a lot of people. Due to the number of decisions people need to make in a day, living on auto-pilot means that they can avoid making those decisions. People have learned to just accept how things are, even if we dislike them. We'd rather not spend the energy or effort in changing things. However, if you are reading this book, I think it's safe to say that you do want to change your life, and you are not happy with where it is at. You are actively making decisions and taking actions to work on your negative thinking and managing your inner critic. The first step that you need to take in this process is to simply just be more curious about the thoughts that occur in your mind. Try to ignite some curiosity regarding your emotional experiences and pay attention to the way you speak to yourself when you are in a conflict or approached by a challenge. This may sound like it's easy but acknowledging your passive thoughts is actually hard since we are so used to living on auto-pilot. Our minds automatically filter out certain things all due to the fact that it knows that you don't like to think about it.

Conclusion

I first want you to give yourself a pat on the back for exercising your growth mindset by learning and reading about all the content in this book. That is a great first step you took by learning more about mindset to reach your long-term goals. Most people have varied misconceptions regarding mindset and the role it plays in your life. I hope that the content of this book has changed your mind regarding this topic, and you now understand that by having the right mindset and making this a regular practice, that you can now find success.

Towards the middle of this book, we spent some time learning about failures. We learned that they are a part of the process of gaining success and that the only way to reach goals is to expect failures and learn to move past them. At the end of this book, we spent more time learning about setbacks and developing a growth mindset. Both of these topics are important in order for a person to achieve their long-term goals. By the time you got to these chapters, I wanted you to have two main takeaways. First, I want you to know that a growth mindset is necessary for success. Without it, you remain stagnant and unable to learn and grow. No one can find success this way. Second, I want you to understand that failures and temptations are everywhere around us. We can do our very best to prevent and avoid them as much as we can but at the end of the day, we must exert our willpower in the face of temptation to reach our long-term goals. Employ goals that you are passionate about so willpower comes more naturally to you.

Next Steps

The next step now is to simply apply these methodologies, tips, and concepts into your reality. Make good goals for yourself that you're passionate about. Break it down into smaller ones and prevent temptation. I promise you that once you get the ball rolling, you'll be able to accomplish more than you have ever imagined.

Where to Go From Here to Keep This in Your Professional Life Practice

Now that you understand and have studied the ways in which to put growth hacking and your growth mindset into practice, all that is left to do is to practice. The saying "practice makes perfect" may seem overused, but it could not be more true, especially when it comes to changing your life.

Description

This book is chock full of information on how to employ the mindset you need to find success in business and in life as a whole! Open these pages to find all the answers you have been looking for in order to find success with your start-up, your career, or any other facet of your professional life!

- What is mindset and how does it affect your life
- How is mindset developed and what affects mindset
- What is Growth Hacking?
- Fear of making mistakes and how it can affect your mindset
- How to change your mindset by addressing your fear of failure
- How can you use Growth Hacking to your benefit in business and in your personal life
- How to be a good leader using a growth mindset and Growth Hacking
- Traits of a good leader
- Non-traditional marketing strategies and how you can begin to think in an innovative and non-traditional way
- How to change your mindset by facing your fears and practicing positivity

Why is it that some people find success at an early age whereas others spend years looking for it but is unable to find it? The simple answer to this is mindset. Your mindset can help you bring not only success in your life in a professional sense, but it can bring you more happiness and life satisfaction. This book will show you how to do this, as it is not a simple process. All you need to bring with you is an open mind and a willingness to learn and grow, as the keyword in this book is *growth!*

It's about building reasonable goals that you are passionate about, building an effective and realistic plan, preventing temptations rather than denying them, and accepting failure with open arms but employing a growth mindset to move past it. This book is full of new concepts that you can begin using today to begin changing your life and improving your success in business and in your personal life, whatever that may entail. By being able to use innovation in business, you will set yourself apart from the rest and will make yourself a great asset to your company or your start-up.

This book is effective in a way that it teaches you realistic and employable habits and techniques that anyone can use to increase their success in business using growth hacking. The concepts are easy to understand and apply as long as the reader keeps an open mind and a learning mindset. An open mind is one that can be molded into anything you like. The opportunities are endless for those who keep it open.

The first step you need to take in changing anything about yourself, especially your mindset, is to start learning more about yourself. The best way to do this is to read a book that can take you from beginning to end, packed full of concepts and information regarding changing one's mindset.

So, don't wait any longer if there are goals you want to accomplish, purchase this book today to begin living a happier and more successful life in business and at home!

www.ingramcontent.com/pod-product-compliance
Lightning Source LLC
Chambersburg PA
CBHW050305220526
45465CB00002B/837